# When Trout Talk

## Fred Carney
## and
## Jim Leason

CHICAGO SPECTRUM PRESS
LOUISVILLE, KENTUCKY 40207

 CHICAGO SPECTRUM PRESS
4824 BROWNSBORO CENTER
LOUISVILLE, KENTUCKY 40207
502-899-1919

Printed in the U.S.A.

10 9 8 7 6 5 4 3 2 1

ISBN: 1-58374-045-7

*Cover designed and illustrated by Joseph Kayse*

# Introduction

For centuries humans have given much thought to the art of taking trout. They have devised contraptions, formulated theories, developed angling strategies, studied the weather for optimum feeding times, attempted to understand how trout think, and spent fortunes on elaborate equipment.

But through the ages, did any of these millions ever consider what the trout might be thinking? For one moment, did they ever stop to think that the trout might be formulating a strategy against them? Were they ever aware that the trout were clued in to their devious little fishing tricks?

Now, in this candid collection of trout thoughts, we take you deep beneath the waters to get a glimpse of the trout's unique vantage point of survival and the environment in which they thrive.

*–Fred Carney and Jim Leason*

# Acknowledgments

To the late Richard Brautigan for his literary works that served as an inspiration for some of our poems and for acquainting us with Trout Fishing in America Shorty (T.F.I.A.S.).

To our family and friends for encouraging us to keep writing and to publish our work.

A note of gratitude also goes to the late Gary Prather for introducing us to trout streams.

This book is dedicated to all fishermen—those still here, those that have left us, and those still to come.

# Contents

# Fish Voices

Although I am unable
To utter a single word,
Within me live two voices,
Which refuse to go unheard.

They are a byproduct
Of instincts formed by time.
It would be nice to speak them,
But I'm as silent as a mime.

One knows that I am hungry,
"Go get that fly up there."
The other warns of danger,
"It could be just a snare."

One screams out loud at me,
"Strike that juicy fly,"
While the other quietly whispers,
"You'd be wise to swim on by."

One spring day they struggled **royal,**
The one said, "Go, go, go."
Now in a creel, gasping for air,
The other says, "I told you so."

I should have listened to the whispers,
But the loud voice was so strong,
As I sink into the darkness
I know the voice was wrong.

Today I swim in the after-life,
And the loud voice has gone away.
But the quiet one still whispers, "Stupid,"
Every second of every day.

# Catching Rainbows

My friend and I went out west
To do the thing that we like best;
Pitching a tent along Frying Pan creek,
Sipping some Jack before we sleep.

Early we rise along with the sun
Ready for fishing, ready for fun,
Wanting to be first with a cast,
Sharing time that would always last.

We didn't know what a hatch was,
And all we had were bluegill bugs.
Do we fish with these, do we dare?
The other trout men could only stare.

No one was catching any fish that day
But the trout men still tried anyway.
Just then my friend got excited, you see,
For a Rainbow had swallowed his busy bee.

For the next ten minutes we felt like thugs
As the Rainbows got hooked on our Kentucky bugs.
We caught our limit in a short time span,
Started a fire and got out the pan.

After the meal, we returned to our camp
As it started to rain and things got damp.
When the rain stopped falling from the sky
A beautiful rainbow caught my eye.

About this time we knew what to do,
Got out the Jack for a drink or two.
We raised our glasses and took a sip,
Toasting the rainbows, and toasting the trip.

# Along The Bank

The sun's reflection off the silver stream
Awakens the trout from nighttime dreams.
It's all so peaceful, or so it seems,
But a storm was on the horizon.

With the sun at his back he came from the west,
Decked out with waders, pole, and vest.
From where I swam he seemed overdressed,
The storm clouds were getting darker.

He eased into the water as pretty as you please.
He didn't go far, just passed his knees,
Opening up his bait box for all to see,
The sound of thunder was upon us.

He chose a fly like it was a long lost friend,
And tied it securely to the leader's end.
He cast his bait in the stream by the bend,
The storm was in full rage.

I tried to avoid that incredible fly
But with all its bright colors it caught my eye,
After swallowing it whole I knew I would die,
I was now in the eye of the storm.

I have to say that I gave it my best
But after a while I had to rest.
He put me in his net that he kept on his vest,
The calm after the storm was starting.

Now the sun came out in the afternoon
After it set, there was a new moon,
My friends all agreed that I died too soon,
Both the storm and I were over.

# Early Morning Movement

Long before the sunrise
A trout man did appear
Sneaking in the moon lit shadows
And getting dangerously near.

The invader was at my front door
Decked out like old Saint Nick,
And if I were to survive the day
I would have to be very quick.

Now this man sat along the bank
To see what the hatch could be,
And glancing over toward a pool
I saw his eye looking straight at me.

At first it made me nervous
And the sweat pored from my brow,
But then I got my fins in gear
And escaped that fool somehow.

However, then he stood erect
With his fly rod in his hand,
Started walking along the stream
Like he was in a marching band.

The trout man cast the fly,
Setting it down next to my head.
If I knew the day was going to be like this
I would have never left my bed.

This trout man has long since gone,
The stream is calm once again,
But I know that when the dawn breaks
Another struggle for life will begin.

# Cast Away

You came to see me again,
I saw you by the water's edge.
You were trying to toss your fly
Close to my rocky ledge.

But once again, you gave yourself away
By stomping around and cussing.
You'll never catch me like that,
You'd wake the dead with all that fussing.

Go ahead, cast till your arm falls off,
I'll just sit over here and laugh.
Your fishing skills, on a scale of one to ten,
Are far below one-half.

I find it especially amusing,
As your line wraps all around you.
When it comes to the game of fishing,
You're lost without a clue.

Come on back, it's good to see you
Wasting your time every day
Standing in the middle of my world
Just casting your life away.

# Life Goes On

Once again, I struck a fly
And once again, I won
The angler was slow to set the hook
With a sore lip, life goes on

I swam around a rotting log
To face a Muskie, which weighed a ton
But a Creek Chub caught his attention
Nervously, life goes on

At another time I struck a fly
And with the hook I began to run
I pulled the line over a razor sharp rock
And with the hook, life goes on

An eagle once had me in his grasp
And was flying toward the sun
When a seagull startled his talons loose
With a great fall, life goes on

I am constantly being preyed upon
And forever on the run
How many times will I get lucky
How many times will life go on

# Swim With Me

Come swim with me through
Grasses wet
And rocks all coated
In green.

Come swim with me around
Dark wedged logs
And through crystal
Waters pristine.

Come swim with me up
My favorite stream
To a place where the flies
Are regal.

Come swim with me where
No man casts
And the cover denies
The eagle.

Come swim with me to
A feeding place
That's like a dream but
Very real.

Come swim with me and
We'll feast together
Where there are no hooks
Of steel.

# Roe vs. Wade

How could she do that,
And scorn the unborn
By laying her eggs
On a path that is worn
With years of travel
By rubber-footed men
Who try to destroy us
Again and again?

She's no kind of mother
To do such a thing,
They can't avoid the waders
And won't hatch till spring.
The size twelve footprints
Will squash them to hell
And to the big-footed stompers
It's all just as well.

Her eggs are already
A treat for our foe,
She's adding more danger
To ensure they won't grow.
If she didn't want them
She could have said so,
There are plenty of trout
Who would adopt all the roe.

She's a slut and a tramp
And she should be fried,
For ensuring the helpless
Will have their future denied.

# Wandering About The Stream

As I aimlessly wander about the pool
I wonder if I'm simply being a fool
To think I can live outside of the school
And outwit the line, hook, and spool.

Being a loner is both good and bad
And for having no friends, I'm no more sad
Than when I swam with Mom and Dad,
Under their eye, I was safe and glad.

But I don't need them; I'm a big fish now.
I'll take care of myself; I'll show them how.
I'm no longer as slow as a lumbering cow,
And through the minnows I'll swiftly plow.

I'll strike, I'll jump, and my belly I'll fill
Till I'm as big as a sow, ready for kill.
But I'll be sure to be cautious until
I've learned enough to dodge the creel.

I think I'll start with that fly over there,
The one with the pretty red and black hair.
It looks like it's sleeping, but I don't care.
Besides, it won't be too easy to scare.

I rev up my fins and pick up some speed,
So as swift as a bullet I can complete the deed.
I hit hard, and swallow, but it tastes like a weed,
Suddenly a victim of my own greed.

As I'm helplessly pulled out of the pool
There's no doubt that I've just been a fool,
To think that I could live outside the school
And forever outwit the line, hook, and spool.

# Waist Deep

Walking along the swift clear stream
With my knee-high waders on,
Looking for some fresh trout to catch,
Searching in the morning dawn.

Looking down stream I see a swirl.
To the untrained it may look like a ripple.
But to this man of seasoned fishing,
It couldn't have been that simple.

I cast the fly toward the fleeing trout.
It landed in front of his face.
He took that fly into his jaw.
That crazy trout didn't even say grace.

It was clear to me the fight was on.
Would the trout win or would I?
Neither one would give an inch.
Neither one wanted to die.

The trout took me deeper into the stream,
As he ripped from the reel more line.
I thought I had the drag set right.
But that was only in my mind.

He took me down to a little pool,
And with a slight grin on his face
He spit the fly right back at me
And quickly put me in my place.

The water was much deeper there.
The trout knew that all along.
He knew that as soon as my waders flooded
I would drown and be long gone.

While under the water, and looking up,
It would come to me sooner, not later.
If given another chance at this life
I would buy a good pair of chest waders.

# The Masters Of The Bait

See the masters of the bait,
So skilled and finely tuned,
See them make deep runners,
See them make a spoon.

See them build their fancy flies
To match any hatch around,
To fool the unsuspecting trout
Into swallowing it all down.

See the masters of the bait
So clever and so cute.
They play with every trout's life,
Like a flutist plays a flute.

See the masters of the bait,
Bend steel to make a hook,
Bringing an end to all the trout,
For the sake of something to cook.

See the masters of the bait,
Wage war on all the fish,
So they can crowd around a table
With fresh catch upon their dish.

# Respect

She came to me in the morning light,
Down the stream and full of fight.
In my waders to my knees,
Fly rod in hand, will do as I please.

I cast my fly and let it settle.
I twitch it some and move it a little.
She looks once and then again,
Enjoys the look but begins to swim.

I feel that we will never meet,
As the stream's coolness surrounds my feet.
Out of the corner of my left eye
I see, once again, she spies my fly.

The fly looking all natural and such,
Waiting for a gentle Brook trout touch.
As she swam from a hidden den,
Seeing the fly, she moved on in.

The strike she made stretched the line.
I knew that this was a trout of its time.
But this trout was worth another look
And after thirty yards she spit the hook.

As she fled from the battleground
Feeling safe and homeward bound,
I looked at her, and she looked at me,
With great respect, we parted company.

# Ole Steelhead

Many think the Steelhead trout
Got its name by changing shade,
But all the trout know otherwise,
Here's how the legend was made.

It goes way back to one dumb trout,
Who didn't want advice.
He had to learn the hard way,
And ended up on ice.

Seems all the old trout had warned him
Of man-made ways to fish,
But he thought that he was crafty
And could dodge the angler's dish.

Then one day a big fat bug
Surfed high upon a wave.
He shoved the older trout aside,
And one hard lunge he gave.

The last thing the others saw
Was his tail fin hit the sky.
He never knew he'd been clobbered
By a skillfully hand-tied fly.

Forever it seems this hardhead's fate
Among the trout was spread,
And somewhere through the ages
His name became steel head.

# Mood Swings

I'm a liberated female
That sure knows her stuff
So I'm not easily scared
By your big macho bluff.

Every spring you show up
With all the latest gear,
But you never seem to learn,
Even year after year.

You like to tell lies of how you
Caught one of my kind
With this bait, or that rod,
Or this type of line.

You read a bunch of magazines
To find which bait is hot
You think the answer is in there,
But guess what – it's not.

You see, I choose the color,
And I choose the bait,
I choose when and how,
So you'll just have to wait.

Your problem is you're insensitive men
And you think you know what is right,
When the truth is this – I'm a female
So I'll bite when I'm ready to bite.

My moods often vary,
And my attitude will flip-flop,
So keep throwing money
At your local bait shop.

Some day all you fishermen
May wake up and see,
To get lucky be sensitive,
And just listen to me.

# Fill The Stream With Flies

Appearing right before my eyes
Newborn, shiny bait arise,
Painfully my stomach sighs,
Fill the stream with flies.

Only brooks will ever know
Why the mono lines don't show,
As my hunger starts to grow,
Fill the stream with flies.

I can't escape the noontime sky.
The glare distorts the dragonfly,
The rapids never seem to die,
Fill the stream with flies.

As I lay in river sleep
With dreams of bait I cannot keep,
Forever locked here in the deep,
Fill the stream with flies.

Place a name upon this stream.
My heart is wet, and it would seem,
Enough to make this poor trout scream,
Fill the stream with flies.

# Barometric Mystery

It's been known for centuries
That we can act in peculiar ways,
We may eat every bug in sight
Or fast for several days.

Smart trout have always pondered
Why our appetites just up and go.
But some trout think it's related to
From where the winds do blow.

One trout said to notice
That when the wind is from the east
We seem to go into a stupor
And will turn down the grandest feast.

Another said that when the wind
Comes howling from the north
That we hunker down in bunches
And none of us go forth.

One trout even noticed,
As she crammed flies into her mouth,
That when she checked the waves above,
They were rolling from the south.

But any trout with half a brain
Knows that winds out of the west
Does something to the flies and hatch
Because that's when they taste the best.

# Fish Shadows And
# How They Wear Them

I was cruising the stream
Early in the morn
Looking for shadows
And how they were worn.

When all of a sudden,
And to my dismay,
I saw two Browns and a Brook
They were heading my way.

They wore the shadows
Of a fish with no fin
Some looked like frogs
All snug in their skin.

Most of these shadows
Were very strange to me
But I'm sure to the trout
They were easy to see.

To have such a shadow
Makes a trout beam with pride,
One that he is content with
Until the day that he dies.

A trout with no shadow
Is like a trout man with no pole,
You just swim around
With no place to go.

Wherever life takes you
Let the stories be heard,
Trout would be embarrassed
If their shadows were birds.

When you see your next Brook
Look to see it's not Bass or Brim,
But a proud trout with a shadow
Designed especially for him.

# Mr. Emmett And Me

Mr. Emmett was a big old Brown trout
Living in Murphy's pond,
The town folks would try to catch him
From dusk until dawn.

They would throw their treble hooks,
And they would throw out their flies.
Some would say they had him,
But that was all just lies.

Each man would rather fish for that trout
Than to make love to his wife.
That was just fine for all the women,
Because it gave them a restful night.

Now I decided to have some fun
With the fishermen of this town.
I went and bought some scuba gear
To hunt Mr. Emmett down.

I found him in the deepest part
Basking in the shade of the dam.
He must have been an Irish Brown
For on his head, he wore a green tam.

I brought him up to the surface
So we could talk trout-to-man.
I told him what I was going to do.
He said, "It sounds like you have a plan."

I brought him to the town square
For all the fishermen to see.
The folks, they came from all around
To take a picture of Mr. Emmett and me.

Now the joke wasn't on the fishermen
Although that's what I told you all.
And Mr. Emmett isn't laughing either,
For now he is mounted on my wall.

# Trout Whine

I hate those slippery rocks
All covered with moss.
The stream is too wide here,
I'm too tired to cross.

Why do the other trout
Get the big flies
When all I ever get
Is silt in my eyes?

It's just not fair
That I get no rest.
I can't even find
A good place to nest.

Those Crappie and Bass
Don't have to jump falls.
Why do I have to
Face those big walls?

After years of struggle,
I sure hate to whine,
But I'll probably end up
An entrée with wine.

# Winter Trout

I find the winter to be the best
For it's the time when I get to rest
With the snow falling from the sky
I know for now I will not fry

The trout men have left for the year
The bears are asleep not far from here
Ice is forming on the water's edge
It's now time for me to vege

The family and I swim with no fear
Because the flies that harm us are not here
The stream itself is clear and cold
It chills the body but not the soul

We want the winter to last, you see
For in the spring we could be history
We have to think and not strike the fly
For if we forget we will probably die

Soon the winter will turn into spring
Trout men will return to do their thing
But for now we will just swim about
Thankful for winter and happy to be trout

# Another View

Looking up from the bottom,
Watching as they swim by,
Knowing that they go places
While I sit and wonder why.

Looking up from the bottom,
Staring up into the light,
Seeing the under bellies of the trout
All proud and very white.

Looking up from the bottom,
Knowing my life rests on sand,
Watching a shadow upon the bank,
Could it be tiny troutman?

Looking up from the bottom,
A different view than from the top,
Sitting all alone at the bottom,
Knowing you're just a rock.

Looking up from the bottom,
Watching trout as they descend.
They tell me stories when they return,
I'm glad to call each one my friend.

Looking up from the bottom,
This is not a bad place to be,
With the help of the trout that I know,
They've given me eyes to see.

# Current News

Unlike the birds that fly above
And communicate with their song,
A trout's only source of news
Is by what comes floating along.

There must be a fire up the way
For I see ash and charred debris.
And Oscar the otter, who's been ill,
Went floating by, heading for eternity.

I saw some cans and a paper cup,
Which tell me the fishing season's begun.
The turtles were out on their logs
Basking in the morning sun.

A bear walked past about a minute ago,
I hope he wasn't looking for me.
Two men in a boat drifted on by,
Trolling a fly that was too small to see.

The water started to get murkier,
I decided it was not time to rest.
When I swam up stream to investigate,
I saw him in his waders and vest.

The hatch was abundant on the surface
And the trout man thought I was blind,
But any trout who keeps up with the news
Would not eat a fly attached to a line.

So the next time you are at a stream
And you think that we trout have no clues,
Just look at what is floating past
And you can keep up with current news.

# Evolutionary Dreams

I'm tired of having to swim upstream
I'm tired of dreaming the elusive dream
That my life will be peaches and cream
When I become a human

I'm tired of swimming and I want to walk
Don't want to blow bubbles, just want to talk
I won't be confined like corn to a stalk
When I become a human

I'm tired of this diet of boring old bugs
I want to have feet to put on soft rugs
I want kisses and lots of warm hugs
When I become a human

I'm tired of the same old banks of this river
I want to make Jello and watch it quiver
All of these things my God will deliver
When I become a human

If I could be granted only one wish
It would be to eat off a fine china dish
Filled with vegetables and fruits, BUT never fish
When I become a human

# Little Trout's Prayer

May the Fish Gods guide me
Through tight fallen limbs
And through hostile waters
Where the mean Muskie swims.

Help me to know
Wrong bait from right,
And should I get hooked,
Give me strength to fight.

Give me the wisdom
To outwit my foes,
Especially the ones
With ultra-light poles.

Instill in me
A keen sense of smell
That I may avoid temptation
And the barbed hooks of hell.

But if I should die
And end up on a plate
Pass on all my parasites
To those that partake.

# My How Flies Time

It doesn't do much good to fuss
About the timing of the fly.
But after months of their disappearance,
I thought I was going to die.

What the hell kind of schedule
Tells them when to come and go?
And obviously, their clocks don't work
When the sky is filled with snow.

My stomach is on a regular beat
Of days and sometimes weeks.
But it never seems to coincide
With the timing of those darned freaks.

I wish they'd get their act together,
Maybe update their ancient clocks.
What do they expect me to live on,
Driftwood, plants or rocks?

Maybe they're dumb and can't tell time,
But I'm sure of one damned thing.
All their alarm clocks go off at once,
And they all show up in spring.

# Stream Signs

Stream signs may not be yellow,
Or reflective in the night,
But a trout must learn to read them,
And must always get them right.

There are no arrows or flashing lights,
Only logs, debris, and sand
To let a traveling trout know
That danger is at hand.

No stop, no yield, no one-way signs
To guide us away from harm,
But the shadow of a big tree root,
With us, will sound alarm.

Still accidents occur each day
When a sleepy trout fails to see
He should have turned left, not right
And slams into a Muskie.

# Uncle Milford

I guess every trout has someone
That likes to tell tall tales
But the lies Uncle Milford told
Were bigger than Humped Back whales.

There was the time he escaped from
A huge three hundred pound man
Who, in anger, was trying to kill him
With a well seasoned iron frying pan.

And who can forget the story
Of how he swam into a submerged car,
Where he locked all the doors and windows
And hid from anglers for an hour.

He told of a time he untied the fly
Of an unsuspecting angler
And replaced it with some moose poop
Just to enjoy the fisherman's anger.

But the biggest lie he ever told
Was about a fight he had with a bear.
And how, after he had whipped him,
The stream was covered with hair.

Uncle Milford is no longer with us,
He was tricked by a fly on a leader.
Now swimming in the big steam above
He's lying to Saint Peter.

# Dancing On The Water

When the hatch was at its best
Us flies would be up before the rest
We dressed inside his fishing vest
And he would put on his waders

Down to the stream we would go
What he would catch we did not know
Could be a Brown, Brook, or Rainbow
As he carefully chose us flies

We were all dressed up in our very best
All tucked away in the fisherman's vest
Just waiting to be put to the test
So we could dance on the water

The old messy ones would try to be neater
So they could be on the end of his leader
Catching the first one, what could be sweeter
Tie me on and give me a throw

On the first cast I would float in the air
Land hard on the water, I did not dare
The other flies would watch and stare
Please let me be appealing

The first strike came hard and fast
It was a big Rainbow that hit at last
The thrill I had, oh what a blast
I was the Fred Astair of the water

I was in his jaw when he set the hook
The Rainbow turned and started to book
He stole the line like he was a crook
I was certainly on a thrill ride

Just about then he rose from the deep
He had fire in his eyes, and it gave me the creeps
He spit me out by the fisherman's feet
And the Rainbow danced off on the water

# Grilled Trout

"I didn't do it,"
The frightened trout said,
As the huge Carp cop
Swam close to his head.

"You're guilty, we know it.
The Sun Perch is dead.
And your slimy little fin prints
Were all over his bed."

His gills began to quiver,
His heart felt like lead
As the ugly police fish's
Face turned blood red.

"Confess, that you did it,"
His screams seemed to spread.
"And I'll see that you get
Some larva and bread.

"But if you insist
On lying, instead
I'll do the one thing
That I know you will dread.

"I'll put you ashore,
You'll be Seagull spread,
And what will be left of you
Won't be more than a thread."

The trout knew he was innocent,
This Carp was misled.
The wrong and injustice
Was now raw and widespread.

But he had been broken,
So guilty he pled,
In hopes they'd return him
To his cool, soft, creek bed.

The Carp cop had hooked him
His chances of release were dead
The scales of justice went against him
And off to a cell he was led.

# Mattie Collins

Mattie Collins was a Rainbow
Who lived at the end of the stream.
A husband and two minnows
Had been her life long dream.

Now the neighborhood she lived in
Was slowly becoming a mess,
The pollution made it a pigpen,
Not a place that should have been blessed.

She worked hard to keep it neat
For her husband and her kids,
But soon she knew that she was beat
From man's pollution and what it did.

Now Mattie had a decision to make,
One that was difficult for her to do.
Taking the lives of her kids and mate
Was not an easy task to get through.

She sent them off in the morning
Each with their own little note.
The words she wrote were very inspiring,
She gave directions to a trout man's boat.

Now her husband and minnows are all gone
Ending up on someone's plate
And Mattie, well, she died all alone,
Finally leaving this polluted state.

Now Mattie Collins had a dream
Not much different than you or I,
But if we don't stop polluting the world
Then man will be next to die.

# Trout Dreams

A dream of jitterbugs
With aquatic dance
Played out in streams
With buoyant prance
Stirred my slumber
Beneath the tall willow
Where a slippery rock
Became my pillow
Until I was jolted
By a strike very sharp
From a bony and useless
Buffalo Carp

# Under The Bridge Blues

Wadding in the shallow waters so swift and cold,
The Rainbow and Brook are there, or so I'm told.
I gaze into the fly box not knowing what to use.
I see the trout sitting there, why am I confused?

I match the hatch the best I can, oh what a lovely treat,
Walking along the little stream with the trout at my feet.
I strip the line from the reel like lightning from a storm.
I can't wait to cast the fly; I know the trout will swarm.

I spot a Rainbow cruising the banks like he was in a car.
The windows were up, the top was down, one door was ajar.
He was sitting in the drivers seat, one fin on the wheel.
As he drove past, the plate said licensed to creel.

I tossed the fly toward his grill, so shinny and waterfall like.
It hit the windshield, broke the glass, the Rainbow took flight.
He went to deeper water; I followed his dim tail lights.
Then I saw T.F.I.A.S. I knew that all would be right.

When we came to the bridge I felt the end would take its toll
On this fast driving Rainbow that was clearly out of control.
His car hit the bridge support making it less than new.
The rainbow colors were all gone, now he was simply blue.

*Trout Fishing In America Shorty (T.F.I.A.S.) is the main character of a book written by Richard Brautigan.*

# As Rivers Rise

My watery home overflows
With contempt for man and plant
And I am elevated with happiness
To see things I normally can't.

I glide through a nylon fabric dome
Stretched tight by plastic poles,
And there's a floating mattress
Now spotted with mud and holes.

Oh look, a rectangle green metal box
Labeled with what?  Oh, Coleman.
It's such a foreign and unusual name,
I get a sense it may be a bad omen.

What's this, a pole with metal rings?
With a round contraption clamped on?
A protruding thread runs its length
And I'm curious to where it might run.

Slowly I follow the thin long lead
Through the last metal ring, then out.
It lies loosely across the fabric dome's floor
Scattered here, there, and about.

I reach the end, which disappears
Beneath a pocketed vest.
I grab a hold to pull it back
And disturb its watery rest.

The murky water begins to calm
And I get a clearer view
Of the surprise that lies in store for me,
Oh, I hope it's something new.

Oh luck of luck it looks like food.
It's my favorite...Mayfly hatch.
But oh, what's this, a shiny point
Concealed in my delicious batch?

I panic and reel back when I recognize
The point so sharp and shiny
My fins rip open the dome's zippered door
And I race to save my hinny.

I hide for days beneath a log
Praying the river will recede to its banks.
And for my narrow little peaceful home
I give the Trout Gods thanks.

# Dropped By For Lunch

As the sun rose, so did I,
Got the kids off, kissed the wife goodbye,
Left the pod, walked on the sod,
It was a good day to stand out.

The morning dew was almost gone.
The flowers were out, singing their song.
A friend of mine was just coming along.
How could a bad day start so good?

The bright colors I had on my bod
Made me the Liberace of the insect squad.
There was nothing that I couldn't do, it seemed,
But I wasn't looking when I fell in the stream.

Floating on top and looking real good,
I tried to escape as fast as I could.
It was to no avail, as I tried to swim,
But then I saw it, the dorsal fin.

The spots on his side let me know he was a trout.
He watched me struggle, as he swam about.
He came from the bottom, and I felt a crunch.
Gulping me down he said, "Thanks for dropping by for lunch."

# How About Them Trout?

Forget the frogs
And Darter Snails,
How about us trout?

And when we get all sensitive
About ecosystems,
Why do you leave us out?

You worry too much about
Salamanders,
What do they know about?

We're higher up on the chain
You know,
So we deserve some clout.

I'll steal your bait
And break your lines,
If you think that we don't count.

Don't make me come over there,
Don't piss me off,
And please, don't make me shout.

So if you need one more cause
To support,
How about us trout?

# No Trout For Cows

It's hard to be a cow
Just eating grass and hay,
To see the sportsmen cast their flies
And haul in trout all day.

Can't cast a line or hold a rod,
Can't begin to open a creel,
Can't pick up worms or tie a knot,
Can't crank the simplest reel.

Waders just won't fit me,
Can't swim to save my life,
Won't even eat a piece of fish,
Afraid of the filet knife.

Why wasn't I born to be like them,
All happy with fish smell.
I watch them scream as they pull one in,
Stuck here in cow hell.

# The Death Of Willy Dumas

I hand-tied Willy Dumas
When I was only ten
And I would like to share with you
All the places that Willy has been.

He went with me to Montana
To catch every trout he could.
He didn't let me down in Vermont,
But I didn't think that he would.

When I was twenty and he was ten
We went out Idaho way,
Fishing streams full of Rainbow,
Catching our limit each and every day.

Now Willy spoke a little French,
So up to Canada we went.
He was hit hard one afternoon
So we left, but his hook was bent.

I put Willy back in the vice
To straighten out the bend.
He was looking pretty raggedy
And I didn't want this to be the end.

We decided to go for one last trip
To catch Brook from a beaver pond.
So off to Big Piney, Wyoming we went
Together for one last song.

For three days we caught our fill
And like a fool I continued to cast
And when the trout took Willy Dumas,
I knew his end was here at last.

# Why Of The Trout

What's our purpose,
why are we here,
why gills and fins,
and not scuba gear?

Why the currents
and not still streams,
why do small bugs
invade my dreams?

Why must I see the sun
through light that's been refracted,
why does every minnow
cause me to become distracted?

I think, oh well, I'm a lucky guy,
as I strike yet another fly,
mine is not to figure why,
mine is but to spawn and die.

# Ice Ceiling

The limbs of winter
Are covered with snow
It blows in the wind
To the cold floor below.
The stream's barely moving
Because of the freeze.
Here, the powers of winter
Will do as they please.
Humans stand up to it,
Riding sleighs down the hill.
They have on warm coats
To ward off the chill.
A lad makes a figure eight
Just over my head.
He's having a ball
While I'm one meal from dead.
I feel sadly imprisoned
By a ceiling of ice.
About now, a fresh hatch
Would taste awfully nice.
I know I can make it
If I focus on one thing,
That winter's death grip
Must give way to spring.
I dwell on one positive
As the cold months go by,
That in all of the stream
There's not one man-made fly.

# Trout Roots

We are of genera **Salvelinus**
and **Salmo,** *some say too,*
We live in nice cool freshwater
and sometime a brackish slue.

To some we are a food source,
to others just a game.
We'd rather just be left alone,
If it's all the same.

In Old English we are **truth,**
In Latin we're known as **tructa.**
Among aquatic vertebrates,
We are definitely pukka.

Every one of us are Pisces,
Not one Taurus among us.
We are friends of all Aquarians
But Cancers make us cuss.

# Wrapped In White Paper Blues

I'd rather be in a stream
Than where I am today,
To be free to swim and eat
With no cares to get in the way.

The place where I'm at now
Is cold but has no water.
My new friends just stare forward,
Some are tall and some are shorter.

To the left of me is some octopus,
To the right some fine frog legs.
Above my head is a big Grouper,
Below me are some Salmon eggs.

My new friends don't stay too long
But others do take their place.
However, they also look stunned
The smiles gone from their face.

One day, I will leave this behind,
I guess when I pay my dues.
I want to go like the proud trout I am,
Not bound, with the white paper blues.

# Evolutionary Rip Off

How did we trout miss the boat
When it comes to evolution?
I suppose it's too late for Mother Nature
To make complete restitution.

Humans used to be short and squatty
But now they're a whole lot taller.
We trout have changed very little.
If anything, we're all now smaller.

Man used to kill and eat with their hands,
Now they go buy groceries, and cook,
While for millions of years we've eaten bugs
And yes, an occasional hook.

They used to crawl like a croc
But now they walk upright.
And yep, we're still swimming
Slow and very uptight.

They used to grunt and groan
And live in dark, dusty caves.
But now they live in mansions
And attend trendy raves.

We evolved with gills and colors,
And these are positive gains,
But we'd trade all our pretty colors
For well developed, larger brains.

# Waterfall Missed

I started out as a fingerling,
In this stream that I call home,
Swimming with all in the school,
Feeling the freedom to roam.

As a teenager in this clear swift stream
I knew that I wanted to date
But with a face of acne and two left fins
Dating would have to wait.

Then when I was twenty-one
Something happened to my stream.
The sludge from the silver mine spilled,
Killing all life in its path, or so it would seem.

Floating upside down on the surface,
Gasping for their last breath of air,
All the trout that I was raised with
Were dying and no one cared.

I fled the scene, swam up the stream,
To escape from the horrors of my past.
Then I came to a place with its own waterfall,
I knew that I had found my home at last.

# Trout Piercing

The old trout just can't understand
Why young trout do weird things
Like tying knots in anglers' lines,
And making surface rings.

But one thing more than all the rest
That make the old ones flip
Is the latest craze of wearing hooks
Pierced through their lower lip.

It must be a rebellious spirit
That makes the young ones sneer
At the deadly, dangerous object
The old ones dread and fear.

The old just cannot understand
Their obvious neglect
For the memory of ancestors
Who are worthy of respect.

They were saying it's the worst
That it has ever been
When a young trout cruised on by
With a bright purple fin.

# The Night Of My 128<sup>TH</sup> Dream

I was wandering around a Montana stream,
The stars fading from the morning light,
Reaching into my vest for just the right bait,
Attaching it to the leader, prepared for the fight.

The fly was picked and cast toward a pool
Where it gently rested on top of the stream.
I twitched it some to make it look real,
But not one trout was here, or so it would seem.

Just as the Neptune King started to salute
At a school of swimming-by fish,
Captain Ahab with harpoon in hand
Prepared to make a whale of a dish.

As we sat down at the supper table,
And tucked our napkins in our lap,
A knocking was heard at the door.
It was a familiar sound of tap, tap, tap.

When the door swung wide open
We all could do nothing but stare,
For in the doorway stood Long John Silver.
He walked over and sat in a chair.

About this time I started to wonder,
Am I still in that Montana stream?
But then the alarm went off in my head,
And I awoke from this trout man's dream.

The fly was still on top of the water,
The wind moved it to and fro,
Then I knew it wasn't a dream,
For I had hooked a huge Rainbow.

# Crossing The Line

When she swam into my pool
She took my breath away.
I couldn't make out her classification
But her skin was reddish gray.

Then she turned and looked right at me
And with her big lips, she made a pucker.
I heard my Mom whisper to Dad,
"There goes the neighborhood, it's a Sucker."

I couldn't take my eyes off her,
She was the prettiest thing I'd found.
Then my Mom caught me looking at her
And started to slap me around.

"They feed off the bottom, you know.
And they'll eat anything they find."
But it was too late; not a word I heard,
I was in love with a fish not my kind.

Within a few days we were madly in love
I knew she was my lifelong mate.
All my trout friends began to avoid me
And look at me through eyes of hate.

But I didn't care; my mind was made up
Because this was the girl for me.
I couldn't believe all the other trout
Didn't see what I could see.

We decided to make our home together
Down by a grove of White Birch.
As I was leaving my Mom whispered low,
"Son, why didn't you just fall for a Perch?"

Many years have passed since the day we met
Now we're accepted by all our kin.
Primarily because our kids are so cute
With their low lips and spotted skin.

# A Trout Runs Through It

The stream is small and not so deep,
Lined with trees tall and fit.
It's a slice right out of heaven,
Happily, a trout runs through it.

The air turns cold, snow appears
And the stream is a frozen pit.
Yet beneath the ice the water flows,
Slowly, a trout runs through it.

The air turns warm, and winter melts,
The stream runs lickety split.
It tosses around heavy logs and rocks,
Carefully, a trout runs through it.

With runoff gone both banks are lined
With anglers seeking a hit.
They form a gauntlet of deadly snares
And frown, as a trout runs through it.

# The Lure's Prayer

Bamboo father whose length is seven
Hollow be thy frame.

Our time has come, thy cast be done
In streams early, around eleven.

Give us this cast, our daily spread
And forgive us our tangles as
We forgive our tanglers.

And toss us not into trepidation,
But deliver us from gravel.

For thou art the ringed one,
And the power, and thrower
Forever.

Amen

# The Streams They Are AChanging

Come gather round fishes
Wherever you roam
And note that the waters
Are tainted with foam
And soon you'll be left
With waste as your home,

For the streams they are a changing.

For Bluegill and Perches
All through the land
Don't swim idly over
The deep poisoned sand
Or else you'll be prey
To the polluter at hand,

For the streams they are a changing.

Come Catfish and Rainbows
Don't crowd the bank
Why settle for water
That's becoming so rank
If we can't make it
We'll end up in a tank,

For the streams they are a changing.

# Snapping Turtle's Favorite Trout Song

*(Everybody Sing Along)*

Ninety-nine trout on a stringer, that's all
A ninety-nine stringer of trout
Bite one off, let's have a ball
A ninety-eight stringer of trout, that's all

Ninety-eight trout on a stringer, that's all
A ninety-eight stringer of trout
Bite one off, let's have a ball
A ninety-seven stringer of trout, that's all

Ninety-seven trout on a stringer, that's all
A ninety-seven stringer of trout
Bite one off, let's have a ball
A ninety-six stringer of trout, that's all

Ninety-six trout on a stringer, that's all
A ninety-six stringer of trout
Bite one off, let's have a ball
A ninety-five stringer of trout, that's all

*(Keep singing until all the trout are gone or your belly is full, whichever comes first)*

# Shallow Waters

I was standing alone in a stream,
And while I was there I had a dream
Of Rainbows, Brookies, shinny and sleek.
The whole dream lasted for a week.

Parts of the dream kept me up at night.
The LSD part was out of sight.
I saw the trout line up, nose to tail,
As it started to rain, and started to hail.

I went to the booth to get the phone
No one was there, just a dial tone.
A Brookie swam by and said, "Hey Jim,
Did you come to fish or to swim?"

Three days later, awake from this dream,
I found myself in the same old stream.
The Rainbows and Brookies were still there
And when I'm gone, will anyone care?

Just as I thought the dream was gone,
T.F.I.A.S. came walking along.
He spoke very little as he went toward the hollow.
He wrote on my back. It said, "shallow water."

# Schools Of Trout And Sunday School

I've spent all of my life going to school
Because that's what all trout do,
But the important lessons about Sunday
Has helped to get me through.

Lessons on Monday through Saturday
Were about breeding, and instinct revival,
But the lessons taught about Sunday
Were strictly about survival.

They taught that Sunday was a day of test,
A day of temptation, not thanks,
A day when the number of anglers
Grew dangerously large on the banks.

We were told it was a day of rest,
A day to be very still,
A day of human tricks and snares,
Designed to maim or kill.

Thanks to the older and wiser trout,
And the lessons learned in Sunday school,
We're all still here to proliferate,
And to pass on our ancient gene pool.

# River Gods A'Riding

When the River Gods go riding
There'll be no more use in hiding
For we all will be abiding
Until the rage starts subsiding.

We know not their source of power.
But they're aroused by a springtime shower.
Snowmelt can also make them sour.
A clap of their hands will make us cower.

We have no way of knowing
When the angry Gods go rowing.
Because their plan is never showing
Exactly when they will be going.

So, we'll just hang on for the ride
And hope to end up with our hide.
And miles away we may abide
After a long and wet, slippery slide.

# Ponds Or Streams

Streams are swift
Streams are cold,
Ponds are still
Or so I am told.

Streams have smooth rocks,
Streams have waterfalls,
Ponds just sit there,
And do nothing at all.

Streams have pools,
Streams have eddies too,
Ponds have banks,
With no money for you.

Streams are full of trout,
Streams are full of hatch,
Ponds are sometimes murky,
You don't know what you'll catch.

Streams are what you fish in,
Streams are what you walk in,
Ponds are what you look at,
Wishing you were in a stream.

Streams are the blood of life,
Streams flow in your mind,
Ponds have shadows on them,
So ponds can tell time.

# Political Trout

He was a small Brown in the big stream of life
With the normal two kids and a Brookie wife.
He lived in the main stream, not in the tributary.
He was truly the catch of the day.

He hung around eddies, waterfalls, and such,
Just trying to find food so he could have lunch.
He would be in the main stream connecting with the hatch.
He was truly the catch of the day.

He liked the pool, stayed away from the fools,
Went to Harvard to be at the top of the school,
Found a bowl for the family to live in,
He was truly the catch of the day.

At the age of twenty-one, the political trout left home.
His gills were full of water, he needed to go roam.
He left his one-eyed Brookie and said, "So long,"
He was truly the catch of the day.

Alone and swimming fast, a fly caught his eye as it passed,
He turned around and gave his fins more gas
So he could catch the demon at last,
He was truly the catch of the day.

# Not One Fly Over
# The Cuckoo's Nest

Bubba Trout's fascination with man-made flies
Was known in and around the river
But in recent times his obsession had grown
And at his madness with fear we did quiver

Apparently some angler had written a message
On every park restroom wall
Saying, for a good time, cast in the river
You're guaranteed to have a ball

Since Bubba couldn't resist a fly
And he had to check out each one
Anglers from all over the country
Came here to have some fun

Flies with sharp hooks lay everywhere
And we couldn't let the kids out to play
So we had to do something with Bubba
And we had to do it today

We decided a frontal lobotomy
Might calm him down a bit
So right between his half-crazed eyes
With a railroad spike, we hit

The anglers left after Bubba's operation
Because his obsession with flies took a rest
Now our river is quiet and safe again
Since there are no flies over that Cuckoo's nest

# Look Alike Trout

Who am I, who are you
Who are we talking about
We are the folks that sit around
And do nothing but talk trout

Who am I, who are you
Does anyone really care
We place the fly in the spot
Do we take our limit, do we dare

Who am I, who are you
Does it really matter
The daily hatch keeps dropping in
And the wannabes keep getting fatter

Who am I, who are you
Do you take only what you need
Or do you take more and more
And leave the stream with less to feed

Who am I, who are you
Wanting more trout that believes
If we kill everything that we have
We will have more wannabes

# Living In The Hatchery With The Mountain Stream Blues

Born in a climate controlled tank
With about a thousand others
Having no real mom or dad
Having no sisters or brothers

If I had been born in a stream
Life would have been better by far
I would have learned to hunt for the hatch
Instead of getting my food from a jar

There is no one here to be chums with
So I stare out the window and dream
My heart it is filled with sadness
For I long to be in a mountain stream

# Little Trout Scout

I was unanimously chosen
To be the school's scout
Because I am bait-wise
And because I am stout

My job is to swim forward
And to keep an eye out
For sharp toothed enemies
And flies floating about

They say I'm important
And that I have some clout
The whole school just loves me
And my skills they don't doubt

I take my job seriously
Some say I'm devout
I'm like an insurance policy
The school can't be without

# Leaving The Stream

I felt it was time to flee the stream
To leave the place where I was raised
To go to new lands, and new water too
To meet new Rainbows and a Brook or two

I felt it was time to flee the stream
To find out what I've been missing
For if you stay too long in one stream
All you will be left with is a dream

I felt it was time to flee the stream
To be the ruler of my own world
So I jumped in the cab with a five-dollar bill
And I told that Carp driver take me over the hill

I felt it was time to flee the stream
To find new waterfalls and eddies too
The driver let me out close to the bend
I tipped him, shut the door and jumped right in

I felt it was time to flee the stream
This water was not as swift or very cold
Eyeing the people from the glass wall within
Watching them eat their food with a grin

I felt it was time to flee the stream
Why does this man have me in his hand
Why am I spilling my guts to this cook
I'm not a Carp or a Bass; I'm just a doomed Brook

I felt it was time to flee the stream
Boy, it's sure getting hotter in here
It's over for dreaming of streams and lakes
For now I'm the main course on this guy's plate

# Insane

Do I care how it might look,
As I swim up to the trout man's hook?
I stare and gaze at the shaft of silver
While other trout just shake and quiver.

Is it not okay to be just me,
A little strange but always free,
Not wanting to be like all the rest
And straying from what's supposedly best?

Now there is nothing that makes me squirm,
Even when investigating a wooly worm,
Knowing that if I take it in my lip,
That I won't be paying for the trip.

I find the trout man's flies pretty you see
And have collected a few for the Christmas tree.
The other trout hide or swim away
I hold up a sign that says, "Try and catch me today."

Some trout come from far away
To see if this will be my last day,
To see again if I can defy the hook
So they can call me a crazy Brook.

But once again I take the chance
To ask the coachman for one last dance.
I got a little closer even for me,
But that's okay for I'm insane you see.

Now after all has been said and done,
I've really had some great fun,
Living, not existing, is for what I strive,
Being insane is my way of feeling alive.

# Down On The Reservoir

The trout men lined the bank like locust
All wanting to be the first to cast.
The trout they stayed in the middle
Taking refuge in the seaweed-like grass.

The sunrise was the signal to start,
As the trout season began again.
The trout were getting nervous as hell
For they were outnumbered by trout men.

As the first fly hit the water
And settled down like a baby in a crib,
The trout they scattered from the middle
Some swam fast while others just hid.

The trout men fished as hard as they could
For the trout that swam below.
Many a Rainbow died that day,
But many were caught and let go.

When the day had ended and the sun had set
And the trout men escaped with the catch,
The trout that remained swam back to the middle
To hide in that seaweed-like patch.

So the next time you fish a reservoir
Don't take any more than you need,
For if you take too many males and females
There will be no trout around to breed.

# Delinquent Trout

Let's go mess
With the Darter Snails
And harass
A few old Chubs.

Then buzz
Those redneck Bluegills
And steal
Their juicy Grubs.

Let's trash a nest
And stir up mud
All around those
Snobby Bass.

Then flip them the fin
And scoot away
Yelling,
"Kiss my scaly trout ass."

# Conservative Trout

Let's do away with federal spending
On shiftless, lazy trout.
There's no incentive to learn new skills
When there's a quick federal handout.

We need to repeal Roe vs. Wade,
Our unborn have a right to live,
So every man, bear and bird
Can enjoy the pleasures we give.

We need new laws that encourage us
To find new sources of hatch,
And tax-codes that will allow us
To keep more of what we catch.

Our young should not be made to deal
With a forced desegregated pool.
They should have the right and freedom
To swim with their favorite school.

One last thing, on which
All trout are sold.
No regulation of charities
That provide larva to the old.

# Bone In My Throat Blues

She came to me in the morning sun.
I set the hook then she was gone.
I placed the fly down once again,
Hooked her good and brought her in.

She had fought a worthy fight,
Still she was going with me this night.
I knew at once I caught a winner,
I also knew I'd have her for dinner.

As I placed her on the plate
She looked so good I could hardly wait.
I tore into her as if she were pumpkin pie,
But then I saw the revenge in her eye.

I took a bite then started to choke
For one of her bones was stuck in my throat.
I couldn't breathe; I was out of my head,
Then I remembered; try eating some bread.

This whole time she still looked at me,
As ghostly a look, as you will ever see.
Her eye started to follow me around the room.
At that point, I sensed my doom.

That night I died choking on that trout's bone.
While in heaven I would sometimes roam.
Came to a stream in the morning light
And it reminded me of that dreadful bite.

# A View To A Homicide

Her dream was a large L.A. stream
And she didn't care what she paid.
She fell in love with a big handsome trout
And he did her in without a doubt

Now this fish was the jealous type,
This we found out near the end.
He still claimed he didn't kill the trout,
And wasn't sure what all the fuss was about.

The big trout said he was somewhere else;
At another stream far, far away,
But then for a reason unknown to most,
He staged a getaway along the coast.

The chase it finally came to a halt.
There was evidence everywhere to be found.
This big trout said he was free of all sins.
However, he was missing one of his fins.

In the court room with his mouthpiece,
Talking like a slick car salesman,
The mouthpiece said, "If I could be so bold,
My client never killed the trout for the gold."

The big trout sat still and said nothing;
He just laughed at us in his own sneaky way.
The twelve sardines that sat in their chairs
Said, "Not guilty," and drew hard angry stares.

Now this big trout is running free.
He's taken a vow to catch the killer.
His search has turned up nothing but ghost
But he claims that he is still looking from coast to coast.

However, this trout wants us to feel sorry
For all his life he has been misunderstood.
To me that's just another lame excuse
For the trout that did the deadly abuse.

So now you've heard the story
Of a little trout who was killed
And the big trout that swims free everyday
And not till he dies, will he finally pay.

# Gone With The Fin

My dog Rhett, who I had bought from a butler,
Tagged along with me to O'Hara creek.
I'd been told to find a pool by twelve oaks
And it seemed that I'd searched for a week.

Stories were told of battles fought here
With a Cutthroat whose markings were scarlet.
Some say the fish had burned down the pride
Of anglers who tried to get him in their net.

I inspected my pole, made from bamboo,
By Tara, a now defunct company,
And rooted around in my box until I found
My favorite fly, the one I call Mammy.

With a long cast, the fly seemed to be prissy
As it danced on a series of small waves,
Then an explosion of surface made me cry out
"You're mine, you'll no longer take slaves."

He surfaced toward me, all scarlet and huge
And I knew with one fault I'd surely be screwed
I screamed aloud to stifle my fear,
"We're bad lots, both of us – selfish and shrewd."

Like Sherman across Georgia he raced
And I tried in vain to bring some line in.
But with the sound of a cannon, the line gave way
And old Mammy was gone with the fin.

I knew all my buddies would never believe this,
They'd say my story was a lie or just a sham,
But I had, in fact, tangled with the scarlet legend
So, frankly my dear, I don't give a damn.

# Hollywood Trout

My friends are all jealous
But I'm not apologetic
For a chance to appear
On National Geographic.

They'd had their opportunity
And were allowed many tries
But during the audition,
They missed too many flies.

I'd kept my mind focused,
Sharp as a steel trap.
I felt good when the director yelled,
"Ok, cut, that's a wrap."

And now I am famous,
With plenty of fans,
And bodyguards to keep me
Out of the pans.

But when they want autographs,
I have to tell them again,
I don't have extended digits,
So I can't hold a pen.

# Little Big Trout

The school had turned
Up a dead-end slue
In search of food
And shade.

But when they turned
To go back to the stream,
They saw the mistake
They'd made.

They couldn't move
There was no place to go,
And their panic began
To spike.

When one small trout
Swam to the front
And studied the
Wall of Pike.

He charged straight on
At the largest Pike
And bit off a hunk of
His tail fin.

The Pike was stunned
And fled from the slue
So he wouldn't be
Bitten again.

The others followed
As fast as they could,
Thinking the little trout
Was crazy.

They'd always thought
That trout were weak,
And dumb, and scared,
And lazy.

The school was safe
With a new trout hero
Who had proved that
He was brave.

So Little Big Trout
Was an Indian name
The school to him
Then gave.

# Siamese Trout

I saw a trout that was pretty strange
For it would swim pointing both ways.
This trout and his twin were joined at the fin,
Each one knowing where the other had been.

Trying to catch this trout with two heads
Was the hardest thing that I'd ever done,
For when the fly was over the brook
Both heads would only just take a look.

Now, I decided how to catch these two,
And went back to the house to get my bamboo.
A thought came to me and I started thinkin',
Could one be asleep and the other be awakened?

Quickly I returned to that swift little stream
To fulfill the finale of the impossible dream,
To catch the trout known as old four eyes,
Neatly tied to my leader were Siamese flies.

I made a false cast then placed it at their faces
They both hit it hard; it was off to the races.
The fight started at nine and ended at half past,
The Siamese trout had been caught at last.

Now what to do next wasn't very clear.
Do I put them back and catch them next year,
Or do I just mount them for all to see?
The answer to this question was confusing me.

The debate I was having was hurting my head
I knew it was time to go off to bed.
But in the morning I knew just what to do,
I invited friends over for a trout or two.

# Out, Trout, And Proud

I've known from my days
As a minnow
That I was unlike
The rest.

While my playmates all
Were macho,
I thought my softer way
Was best.

They'd swim and chase
And fight for food,
While I found beauty
In the stream.

I suppose that I had
An artistic eye,
Or at least that's how it
Would seem.

I didn't spread my sperm
On eggs,
But my buddies to them
Would rush.

And when I saw
A big male trout
My gills would burn
And flush.

I'm no longer ashamed,
But proud,
Of the freedom
I now know.

And there's nothing better
In the whole wide world
Than a strapping, young
Male Rainbow.

# Troutanic

She was the talk of all the rivers.
She was massive, yet sleek and nimble.
Her colors flashed like neon lights
And it was said she was uncatchable.

Others traveled from miles around
To view this aquatic wonder.
When she swam beside their gatherings
Her size, they all would ponder.

She was the pride of high society.
Finally, a trout no man could land.
Some said even God couldn't catch this fish
Because she was so powerful and grand.

She boldly swam full stream ahead
With no thought of man-made wrath,
But she failed to see the over-sized fly
Floating quietly within her path.

The instant that she saw it,
She swerved left to miss the hit.
But she struck it with her right side,
And deep the huge barb bit.

The others watched with disbelief
This scene they thought couldn't occur.
Within an hour she slipped away
And their pride, she took down with her.

# Big Boned Trout

My trout girlfriend
Told me she was fat.
But, my amorous skills
Were honed.
I told her she wasn't fat at all,
That she was simply
Big boned.

But my words
Didn't help her
And she swam away.
Yeah, she's a little chubby,
But what's a guy
To say?

She'd swam laps, worked out hard,
And ate not one
Fat bug.
But, it seemed my
Fins got shorter
With each, and every, hug.

I couldn't console her,
So she left our
Honeymoon pool
In search of full acceptance
In a well-stocked,
Bigger school.

Later that week
I saw some men
Cleaning one of my own.
Imagine my horror when
One guy said,
"This darn trout's all bone."

# The Velvet Frog

I swam past the cans of Tuna,
I swam past the waterfalls,
I saw you talking with a stranger,
A little Brookie was in danger.

I swam out on the lawn,
I swam out to get the pill,
I heard the music and saw the band.
The man had a fly rod in his hand.

I went to the alley to bowl a few,
I had on my shadow, but then it flew,
I talked to a man, his name was Stan,
He was putting on a Royal Coachman.

I saw a stream that was a neon sign,
I saw a sign that was a neon stream,
I saw the fly ease down in the water,
Do I warn the Brookie, you think I otter?

I saw the light reflect in the pool,
I saw T.F.I.A.S., that was pretty cool.
I saw the Brookie eyeing that fly,
Any second now the Brookie would die.

I have seen the stream of life and death,
I have wadded in the coolness of its breath,
I have danced on the water and on the moon,
But the Brookie didn't know death would come so soon.

# Twist And Trout

Well set the hook baby now (set the hook, baby)
Twist and trout (twist and trout)
C'mon, c'mon, c'mon, c'mon baby now (come on baby)
Come and work me on out (work me on out)

Well, work that line out sonny (work it on out)
You know you cast so good (cast so good)
You know you got me running now (got me running)
Just like you knew you would (like you knew you would)

Well, take the slack out baby now, (take the slack out)
Twist and trout (twist and trout)
C'mon, c'mon, c'mon, c'mon baby now (come on baby)
Come on and work me out (work me on out)

You know I'll twist and twirl (twist and twirl)
You know I'll twist so fine (twist so fine)
You got me twisting closer now (twisting closer)
And I hear you say, "You're mine." (hear you say, "you're mine")

# Leaf Me A Lone

Leaf me a lone Oak,
For the season is neigh
To clothe nature's giants
Up high, to the sky.

Leaf me a lone Oak
And I'll swim nearby.
Leaf me a lone Oak
To befriend the new fly.

Deep in its shelter
I'll suspend down below
To see what's delivered
By the slow, even flow.

Beneath the green giver
I'll rest for a spell
To see what will drop
As its long arms unveil.

I know I can trust it
It always provides,
And nothing it holds back,
And nothing it hides.

Leaf me a lone Oak,
I'll be one happy trout.
Leaf me a lone Oak,
Not a coniferous sprout.

# Ghetto Trout

Don't nobody want
To live in our hood,
And I really don't know
Why we think that they would.

Things here be bad
For the young and the aged.
Your trout markings don't matter,
In this dump you'll stayed caged.

We're living off handouts
And suffering the pangs
Of substandard bait
Left by bottom-feeding gangs.

All that we dream of
Is a chance to stand taller,
And like Bluegill, and Sunfish,
Get an occasional night crawler.

# Going Down The Pike
# With Rochester

Rochester and I go back a long way
For we both were born on the same day.
We had different moms so it appears
But our dad was the same, that's what we hear.

Where ever we went we went as a pair
Be it at a street light or in someone's hair.
I'd be next to Rochester or he next to me
We would be side by side for all eternity.

One day we were flying high above the trees
When Rochester looked over and said to me,
"I think I will land on that lake for a drink."
I said, "Hurry back," and he was gone in a blink.

I watched as Rochester flew faster and faster
Heading for the lake, heading for disaster.
I started out after him in a downward spin,
For from my perch I had spotted the fin.

We both hit the water at about the same time.
I looked at Rochester, and he said he was fine.
I told him that we would have to leave here
For that fin that I saw was getting dangerously near.

About that time my body turned blue
As Rochester and I were cut in two.
The Pike's teeth were sharp and wouldn't release.
We died in his stomach, and now we're at peace.

# Loosey Laker

Five fathoms down she patrols the deep,
A breathing agent of stealth.
Having overcome a thousand enemies,
She's forty-five pounds of health.

Her greatest threat is from above.
She knows that trollers wait
With fancy gear and braided line
To sink their deep-running bait.

Her eye is trained but in the dark
Real bait and lures are twins.
To the trollers joy she often errs,
But to their sadness, she always wins.

Seasoned trollers can't keep her on,
To this day she's foot-loose and fancy-free.
After years of lost line and lures
They refer to this laker as Loosey.

# No More Salmo

Every species has a label
So scientists can look real smart,
But from the group that they put us in,
We'd just as soon depart.

They say we are salmoniform,
Which means we are related
To stupid, clumsy Salmon
Who, by us trout, are very hated.

We can live with Salvelinus
Or maybe Oncorhynchus,
But to think they call us Salmon
Is enough to make us cuss.

We're Rainbows, Brook, and Cutthroat,
Not Sockeye, Chinook, or Pink
That are dumb enough to be put in cans,
And when opened, really stink.

We are harder to catch, and prettier
Than those who are canned, and common,
You can call us Dolly Vardens,
But just don't call us Salmon.

# Talking Trout Trash

There was a time when
We could glide
Through the steams
Without the fear

Of running into a
Firestone tire,
Or getting cut by
A can for beer.

We'd watch the surface
For danger there,
Not look below
For junk.

But now we have to
Watch both sides
Lest we swim into
A trunk.

Refrigerators, washers,
And furniture too
Lay within
Our swimming paths.

Headlights, bottles,
And old windshields
Form a hazardous maze
Of glass.

We no longer fear
The angler's
Art, his rod, and reel,
And creel.

We're now afraid
That if things don't change
We'll be living in
A watery landfill.

# Air Express

The day started out like all the rest
Searching for the unsuspecting hatch.
Seeking one who was good and fat
One who was slow and easy to catch.

After the success of my morning meal
I decided to cruise to the waterfall,
Passing the others on their quest for food,
Saying good morning to one and all.

Returning from my trip downstream,
Slipping through the current with great pride,
Once again looking for someone to eat,
Then feeling a sharp pain in my side.

At first I thought it was an appendicitis attack,
The pain was so fierce that I cried.
But as I was lifted from the stream that I loved,
I saw the eagle and knew what was in my side

Soaring higher from the only home that I knew,
Watching as my world became a mess,
Quickly turning my attention to the rocky ledge
And seeing two small eaglets waiting in the nest.

The eagle gently laid me between them
As I tried to escape by flopping around.
But from this lofty perch so high,
If I succeeded I would die as I hit the ground.

Now the birds made quick work of me,
Leaving nothing but my fins and my tail.
As thoughts came back of my morning meal,
Like the hatch, I was destined to fail.

# Trout The Ripper

A legend thrives in stories told
From Wisconsin to Tibet,
Of one strange trout that has struck all baits,
And eluded the angler's net.

Some trout claim they know him,
Others say they're kin,
Some say they just saw him,
While others wink and grin.

He's the emboldened terror of waters
That likes to strike at dawn.
He's the curse of angler's fancy,
And plays them like a pawn.

They say he comes from nowhere
With no ripples, wave or splash
And rips the flies from leaders
Then is gone in just a flash.

They say you can hear him laughing
Where men wade rocky streams.
He's the Zorro of the watery world
That haunts the angler's dreams.

No one knows what tribe he's from,
If he's Rainbow, Brown or Brook,
But he exists in the mind of every fish
As a hero that destroys the hook.

# Brookie Boulevard

Frying Pan Creek, the Snake River too
These are but just a few
Waterway highways that trout travel each day,
Some for work, some for play.

At the Firehole River you will see them there
Sitting at the stop light combing their hair,
Watching as the others go swimming by
Knowing that some will live, and some will die.

Little Brown's Creek, it was stocked to the gills
With all sorts of fish and with all of their frills.
He drove up on the Santa Monica Freeway,
In a salmon Caddie on his very last day.

At Sinking Creek, the Rainbows came in droves.
There were so many they were placed in rows.
The red lights were flashing and the cop was a toad.
There was a trout crash on a lonesome dark road.

Up at the Wabash the news came in fast
Of the Rainbow trout that died in the crash.
I felt sad for his widow that he left behind
For he was truly a trout who died before his time.

Standing in the water of the North Platt River,
With fly rod in hand I started to shiver.
When the fly landed, line stripped out by the yard
I knew I was in the fast lane of Brookie Boulevard.

# Skinned-Head Trout

"Trout power, trout power, trout power," they yelled,
As they swam around the school of Bluegills.
"Don't share our stream with worm eaters," they cried,
"The only good Bluegills are the ones in the creels.

"You might find our pictures in the same books,
But that's as far as it goes.
They can't force us to live together.
How this got started no one knows.

"We were here first and you were imported,
You bobber-loving jerks.
You're ugly, and pudgy, and embarrass us all
With your stupid little baitfish quirks.

"Trout power, trout power, trout power," they cried,
"We must act before it's too late.
Bluegills are a disease that will consume us all.
It's a matter of survival, and not just hate."

# The Garlic Cheese Blues

I'm a proud Cutthroat, as you can see,
And trout men have thrown all their hooks at me,
But the strangest one that I ever did see,
Was all covered up with garlic cheese.

Now my friends told me to eat it all,
For that garlic cheese would lower my cholesterol.
I'm not real fat nor am I too thin,
But they didn't tell me of the hidden hook within.

I took that cheese and began to chew
And after one bite, I think I knew,
The cheese was covering that golden shaft
And my friends were having the last laugh.

About that time I shook it free from my lip
I said, "So long and have a nice trip."
I swam by the bank and watched it float away
Knowing full well that we would meet again someday.

Now as I patrol the stream for food
I don't want to seem ungracious or rude.
Don't try to temp me with that yellow sin
For I will never go after garlic cheese again.

# Trout Ride

Keep movin,' movin,' movin,'
Though the flies we're disapprovin'
Keep us trout a movin,' Trout ride.
We'll never understand 'em,
Men cast, throw, and land 'em.
Soon they'll be casting high and wide.
My heart's a calculatin,'
That real hatch will be waitin,'
Be waitin' at the end of my ride.

Swimmin' on, headin' up,
Headin' up, swimmin' on,
Swimmin' on, headin' up, Trout ride!
Headin' out, floatin' in,
Floatin' in, gettin' out,
Net 'em out, float 'em in, Trout ride!

Keep rollin,' rollin,' rollin'
Though the streams are swollen,
Keep us trout a rollin,' Trout ride.
Through drought and wind and weather
Crazy anglers, or whatever,
Wishing some hatch was by my side,
All those things I'm missing,
Safe waters and bugs hissing
Are waiting at the end of my ride

Swimmin' on, headin' up,
Headin' up, swimmin' on,
Swimmin' on, headin' up, Trout ride!
Headin' out, floatin' in,
Floatin' in, gettin' out,
Net 'em out, float 'em in, Trout ride!

# Hooked On Flies

Some say that it's an addiction
That you will never outgrow,
And when a new spring arrives
The trout show up in droves.

The new life that appears to us
To trout men is known as the hatch,
But to the trout that swim in these waters
It's a tasty treat that can't be matched.

As you watch the frenzy that unfolds,
The trout tearing the flies apart,
The massacre that has happened here
Won't be finished until after dark.

Now the trout strike without any fear
Filling their bellies before they spawn,
But the mothers of the new hatch know
That most of their offspring will soon be gone.

When the day of carnage has ended
And the trout have settled down to rest,
A seasoned trout man gives a chuckle
As he puts on his fly fishing vest.

As the new day begins on the stream
And the trout return for another meal.
The trout man ties on his best fly.
The fly that is made from feathers and steel.

He cast his fly into the middle of the hatch
He had no doubts or misconceptions
Just then a huge Rainbow took the fly
And the reason he took it is fly addiction.

# Spotted Trout

I was ice fishing long ago.
What steam it was, I do not know.
My feet were cold, wet and damp.
The stream was running toward my camp.

It trickled down from the forest floor,
Down the mountains and much more.
The stream had both body and soul.
A lady was there with a fishing pole.

She had been to Alaska, so it would seem,
In search of the perfect trout-filled stream.
In the back of her car she had two rods.
A passerby saw this and gave her two nods.

The stream continued on its way
Stocked with trout all at play
It seemed to flow toward flat land
It slowed as it reached a beaver dam.

This stream was full of the hatch
Lots of trout, easy to catch
The lady soon filled up her creel
No luck for me, I'm fishing still.

The part that was missing from this stream
Came to me in the middle of a dream
It had eddies, waterfalls, rocks, and trees
But Spotted trout were not to be.

# The Catch

Wadding in the stream of my life
Hoping for a record trout
Eyeing my flies in the box
Picking the one that had clout

As the line zipped from the reel
And the fly gently settled to rest
I knew if I were to reach my dream
Then I would have to be at my best

The current took my fly downstream
To a small pool in the bend
And when the Rainbow struck it
I didn't want this fight to end

I played this trout for over an hour
And he tired as he went in my net
As I held him up to take a look
This trout was so beautiful, I wept

He was the record that I hoped for
But it came to me this was wrong
I took a mental picture of this trout
Put him back in the stream and he was gone

# Wet Or Dry

The dilemma that we face
When we first step into a stream
Is what will attract the trout
What flies did we fail to bring

As we gaze into our fly box
And confusingly scratch our head
Should we use a Gray Ghost
Or an Innis Stone instead

Some like the feel of a Black Ant
Others like the Buckskin Crawdad
Having all these pattern choices
As a fisherman makes me glad

So it doesn't really matter
Which fly that you finally chose
The fact that you are fishing
Will chase away your blues